# CREEPY CRITTERS OF THE SOUTHWEST

**Western National Parks Association**
TUCSON, ARIZONA

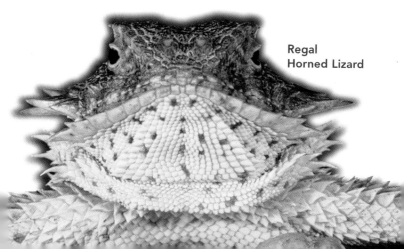

Regal
Horned Lizard

**W**HAT COUNTS AS A CREEPY CRITTER? In this book, it's something that sends a shiver down your spine or stops you in your tracks.

All thirteen of the critters described on these pages are known to have those effects—especially on people who don't know the critters very well. Once people learn about these so-called "creepy critters," their fear is often replaced by feelings of respect, gratitude, or sheer awe.

In the natural world, being creepy can be a good thing. It can give some animals special advantages over others. For example, take the Gila monster, described on page 9. Its creepy skin coloration sends a message to predators, telling them to back off and leave this venomous reptile alone.

Keep in mind that many creepy critters only *look* scary. Most actually

Desert shrew

perform important tasks for the environment. Bats, for instance, eat pesky mosquitoes. They also pollinate plants. Without these winged mammals, our world would be an uncomfortable place.

Remember that all wild animals can be dangerous, especially if frightened or handled roughly. For this reason, never treat wild animals as if they were pets.

Read this book and you will gain a new appreciation for bats, rattlesnakes, armadillos, and other creepy critters that make their homes in the forests, fields, and deserts of the Southwest.

# ARMADILLO

The ancient Aztecs of Mexico called this critter *azotichli*—a name that means "turtle-rabbit." That's a fitting description for this hare-sized mammal with a leathery, jointed shell. Our name, *armadillo*, means "little armored one" in Spanish. ◆ The nine-banded armadillo is an oddball. Unlike other armadillos, it can't roll into a ball to protect its soft belly, when threatened. Instead, it chooses to run away or, if cornered, to dig its way underground. See? Those wicked-looking claws are for digging, not fighting. ◆ Could an armadillo bite a person? No, not even if it wanted to. Its small, knobby teeth are for munching on insects, worms, and other small, live foods.

# TARANTULA

What has eight eyes, blue blood, huge fangs, and four pairs of long, hairy legs? The answer is the tarantula. Tarantulas are the largest spiders in the world. Tarantulas hunt at night, seldom straying more than a few yards from their homes—small burrows in the dirt. Despite their large size, most are gentle and meek. But beware! Tarantulas will bite if you pick them up.
◆ Many people are afraid of tarantulas and other spiders. Their fear, called *arachnophobia*, (uh-RAK-ni-PHOB-ee-uh) is unreasonable but real. Only the tarantulas' prey—mainly insects—should be fearful of these gentle giants.

# TARANTULA HAWK

Meet the tarantula hawk— a two-inch-long wasp that tangles with critters twice its size. This insect attacks giant spiders. When a female finds one, she quickly jabs it, paralyzing it with venom from her needle-sharp stinger. Think *that's* nasty? What's next is worse. The tarantula hawk lays an egg on the spider's abdomen, and when the egg hatches, the baby (called a larva) feeds on the still-living spider's flesh. It munches for weeks on the dying spider, feasting until it is fully grown. ◆ The sting of a tarantula hawk is very painful. Lucky for us, these wasps rarely sting people. They'd rather use their venom to get food for their young.

# SONORAN DESERT TOAD

The Sonoran Desert toad has a secret in its skin—a toxin that can weaken or kill any animal that tastes or touches it. That and the toad's great size give it the freedom to wander where it pleases. Most active at night, this warty wonder likes to lurk beneath streetlamps and porch lights, waiting for moths and other light-loving prey to appear. Not picky, these toads will eat practically anything they can cram into their mouths—moths, grasshoppers, centipedes, scorpions, small lizards, mice and, yes, even other toads. You can hear these toads trilling with gusto after a good rain.

# TURKEY VULTURE

Its red, featherless head and sharp, hooked beak give the turkey vulture a creepy look. Just as strange to us is this bird's diet of rotting meat. A strong sense of smell helps the turkey vulture locate its next stinky meal. That may sound disgusting to you. Still, turkey vultures perform an important job. If it weren't for these and other scavenging animals, the land would be covered with dead and dying animals. By disposing of road kill and other forms of carrion, the vultures help to clean up our planet.

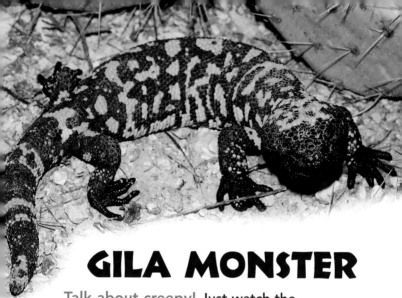

# GILA MONSTER

Talk about creepy! Just watch the low-riding Gila monster as it creeps across the land. Up to 22 inches in length, this critter is the largest lizard in the United States. It spends most of its time out of sight, resting in a burrow below ground. The orange and black patterned scales of the Gila monster send a message to other critters, including humans, a message to "look but not touch." That's because the Gila monster is one of only two venomous lizards in the world. For safety's sake, it's best to leave this mega-reptile alone.

# RATTLESNAKE

Southwestern deserts and mountains are havens for rattlesnakes. These fanged reptiles are skilled hunters. The largest ones track down rabbits and birds, while the smaller kinds are content with lizards, mice, and other more delicate fare. To kill its prey, a rattler will strike and inject its lethal venom. Then it waits for its dinner to die. ◆ Rattlesnakes attack people only in self-defense. The rattler will try to avoid such a confrontation. If it can't hide or slither away, it will coil its body and shake the rattle at the tip of its tail. With luck, the loud buzzing of the rattle will frighten away the two-legged intruder.

# SCORPION

Millions of years ago, giant-sized scorpions lived in the sea. Today, their much smaller relatives live on land, often far from water. Scorpions feed on insects and other small animals, capturing their prey with their two large front claws. A hungry scorpion jabs its victim with the thorny stinger on the tip of its tail. Poison flows through the hollow thorn, swiftly paralyzing or killing the prey. That may sound cruel but, hey, a scorpion must eat to survive! Even the meanest scorpions would rather hide than pick a fight with a person. That's a good thing—the stings of a few scorpions are potent enough to kill human beings.

# BATS

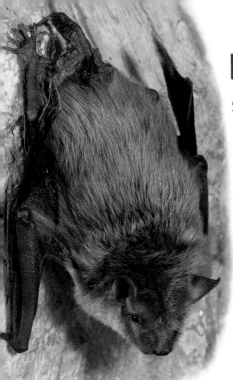

Some people think bats are scary because they flap around at night. But those in the know understand that bats make our world a better place. Take brown bats, for instance. One of these winged mammals can gulp down a thousand mosquito-sized bugs in an hour! ◆ Some bats are pollinators. They carry pollen from plant to plant as they feed, which helps many fruits grow. Others pass the seeds from the fruits they eat, helping plants spread their seeds far and wide. ◆ So what if bats look like flying mice? We'd be sad, bug-bitten, and hungry if all southwestern bats were suddenly to disappear.

# GREAT HORNED OWL

Beware of those large glowing eyes peering out from the darkness. Well, only if you're a small bird or mammal, that is. The largest owl in the Southwest is a very good hunter, catching and eating rabbits, hares, squirrels, ducks, pheasants, and even smaller owls. Specially shaped feathers help the great horned owl fly without making a sound. This helps the hungry owl mount a sneak attack. After eating, the owl upchucks a tidy package (called an owl pellet) with any bones, feathers, or fur it can't digest.

# GRASSHOPPER MOUSE

This critter's been called a coyote in mouse's clothing. That's because the six-inch-long grasshopper mouse acts like a coyote, only on a much smaller scale. Like a coyote, the grasshopper mouse is a predator. It feeds mainly on insects and the occasional mouse or vole, killing its prey with a swift bite to the neck. When threatened, this rascally rodent rears up on its hind legs, points its nose to the sky, and howls—just like you-know-who. Its shrill cry is only a second long but you can hear it half a block away.

# JAGUAR

Although it's the largest cat in the Americas, the jaguar is shy of humans. It has good reason to be cautious. As the first Spanish settlers moved into the region, *el tigre* lost its hunting grounds to cattle ranchers and farmers. By the early 1900s, the jaguar had all but disappeared from its former range. Today, we rarely see jaguars in the United States. Recent sightings are probably cats that have wandered north from Mexico. An adult jaguar can weigh 300 pounds and measure eight feet from its nose to the tip of its tail. Despite their large size, they can still sneak silently across the landscape, taking other large mammals by surprise.

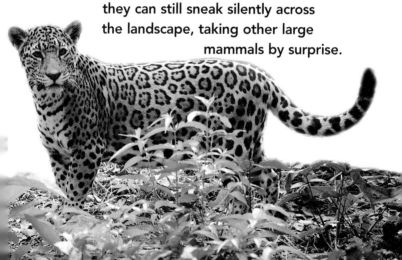

# COMMON POORWILL

The poorwill's name comes from its call—
"poorwill-poorwill-poorwill-poorwill." Active only
at night, this bigmouth is more often heard than
seen. Poorwills belong to a group of birds called
goatsuckers. Long ago, people thought these
critters drank milk from the teats of goats! ◆
Today, we know the poorwill feeds on
insects. It nabs these small morsels while flying
with its mouth open wide. During cold winter
months, when food is scarce, poorwills become
motionless, remaining that way for months. No
wonder that the Hopi Indian's name for the
poorwill is *hölchokoor*, "the sleeping one."